# DELIVERING GREAT CUSTOMER SERVICE

## PUT YOURSELF IN THEIR SHOES.

**NOE TOVAR-MBA**

**PUBLISHED BY**
**NOE TOVAR 2023**
**AMAZON**

SCAN FOR AUTHOR PAGE TO ACCESS
OTHER BOOKS BY THIS AUTHOR

For more information, and other titles by this author please scan QR code on previous page.

ISBN: 9798861267861

Imprint: Independently published

# Table of Contents

# Dedication

This book is dedicated to my family, whose unwavering support has been the bedrock of my journey, and to my friends, who have been both critics and confidants, thank you for being the pillars that held me up when the words threatened to crumble.

To the late nights and early mornings, to the moments of inspiration and the struggles of doubt, this dedication is a testament to the rollercoaster of emotions that accompanies the creation of every written word.

May this book serve as a token of gratitude to all those who have touched my life and inspired me to put my thoughts and experience to paper to share what I know and what stirs my curiosity. Your influence is woven into the very fabric of these pages, and I hope that the research, experience and personal thoughts within resonate with the same warmth and wonder that your presence has brought to my world.

With heartfelt appreciation,

With admiration and gratitude,

Noe Tovar-MBA

Each chapter in "Hustle Smart, Not Hard: Maximizing Efforts for Maximum Results" delves into essential strategies and practices to help readers optimize their efforts, achieve their goals, and attain sustainable success in their pursuits.

# CHAPTER 1

# INTRODUCTION

In the bustling city of New Haven, where dreams are chased relentlessly and success is the ultimate prize, a young entrepreneur named Alex finds himself immersed in a whirlwind of challenges and opportunities. Fueled by ambition and a burning desire to make it big, he embarks on a journey to carve his path in the competitive world of business.

In this fast-paced, ever-changing landscape, the age-old adage of "working hard" seems like the only path to success. But as Alex soon discovers, there's more to the equation than just sheer effort. Guided by the wisdom of an enigmatic mentor, he begins to unravel the secrets of "Hustle Smart, Not Hard."

Within the pages of this tale lies a profound revelation that defies conventional beliefs. Alex learns that true success isn't solely about burning the midnight oil but rather about strategically maximizing efforts for maximum results. Armed with this newfound understanding, he sets out to navigate the intricacies of time management, productivity hacks, and leveraging the power of collaboration.

As he encounters unexpected setbacks and triumphs, Alex realizes that the true essence of hustling smart lies not in mere shortcuts or quick fixes, but in cultivating a mindset that prioritizes efficiency, innovation, and continuous growth.

In "Hustle Smart, Not Hard: Maximizing Efforts for Maximum Results," embark on a riveting journey alongside Alex as he unravels the secrets that propel him toward unprecedented heights of success. This book sets the stage for an inspiring tale of self-discovery, resilience, and the art of balancing ambition with wisdom – a story that will leave you questioning your own approach to achievement and pushing you to redefine what it truly means to hustle smartly.

# Embracing the Hustle Smart Mindset

Welcome to "Hustle Smart, Not Hard: Maximizing Efforts for Maximum Result." In this book, we will delve into the transformative concept of hustling smartly, an approach that challenges the traditional notion of working tirelessly to achieve success.

Gone are the days when the hustle was synonymous with burning the midnight oil and sacrificing all aspects of life for our goals. In the pages ahead, we will explore how to embrace a more balanced and effective approach to achieving our aspirations.

In this introductory chapter, we will discuss the core principles of the Hustle Smart mindset and its potential to revolutionize the way you approach work, productivity, and personal growth. We'll discover that hustling smartly is not about taking shortcuts or compromising quality; rather, it's about leveraging your time, energy, and resources to their fullest potential.

Get ready to unlock the secrets of smart hustling and discover how to achieve maximum results with less stress and more fulfillment.

Let's embark on this journey together and transform the way we approach success and productivity. Are you ready to embrace the Hustle Smart mindset? **Let's dive in!**

# Hustling Smart vs. Hustling Hard

In today's fast-paced and competitive world, the concepts of hustling smart and hustling hard often come into play when pursuing our goals.

Hustle smart, not hard" is a mantra that emphasizes the importance of working intelligently and efficiently to achieve maximum results. It encourages individuals to focus on strategic efforts rather than simply putting in long hours without a clear plan or purpose. By adopting this approach, one can optimize productivity and effectiveness in both personal and professional endeavors.

The concept of "hustle smart, not hard" is based on the understanding that not all efforts lead to equal outcomes. Merely working hard without a well-defined strategy can result in wasted time and energy. On the other hand, employing a thoughtful and calculated approach can yield better results with less expended effort.

Let's explore the key differences between these two approaches:

**Hustling Smart:**
1. Strategy-driven: Smart hustling involves careful planning, goal setting, and prioritization. It focuses on creating a well-thought-out roadmap to achieve desired outcomes efficiently.

2. Resource optimization: This approach emphasizes making the most of available resources, whether it's time, energy, or technology. It seeks to leverage these resources effectively for maximum impact.

3. Adaptive mindset: Smart hustlers are open to learning, adapting, and iterating on their

strategies. They are willing to adjust their course based on feedback and new information.

4. Work-life balance: Smart hustlers recognize the importance of maintaining a healthy work-life balance. They prioritize self-care and well-being, knowing that sustained success requires taking care of oneself.

**Hustling Hard:**
1. Effort-focused: Hustling hard is characterized by putting in extensive effort and long hours to achieve goals. It often involves a relentless pursuit of success, sometimes at the expense of personal well-being.

2. Persistence and determination: Hard hustlers are known for their unwavering determination and resilience in the face of challenges. They are willing to work tirelessly to overcome obstacles.

3. Sacrifices: Hustling hard may require sacrificing personal time, hobbies, or

relationships to focus solely on professional pursuits.

4. Results-driven: While hard hustlers are driven by results, the approach may not always be as efficient as smart hustling, leading to potential burnout and decreased productivity.

Ultimately, the key lies in striking a balance between these two approaches. Hustling smartly allows us to achieve results with greater efficiency and satisfaction, while still maintaining our well-being and happiness along the journey. Remember, success is not just about how hard you hustle, but how strategically you hustle.

# Understanding the Importance of Efficiency

Efficiency is a fundamental concept that pervades various aspects of our lives, from daily tasks to complex systems and organizations. At its core, efficiency refers to the ability to achieve maximum output with minimum wasted effort, time, or resources. Understanding the importance of efficiency is crucial as it directly impacts productivity, sustainability, and overall well-being.

In today's fast-paced world, where time is a valuable and limited resource, being efficient allows individuals and businesses to accomplish more in less time. Whether it's completing tasks at work, managing personal responsibilities, or pursuing hobbies, efficiency enables us to use our time more effectively, giving us the opportunity to focus on other important aspects of our lives.

Merely working hard is not always enough to guarantee success. Smart hustling, on the other hand, involves the strategic and efficient use of our time, resources, and skills to maximize productivity and achieve desired outcomes.

Efficiency is the key to unlocking the full potential of smart hustling. It is about doing things in the most effective and optimized way, saving time and energy while producing exceptional results. When we combine hustle with efficiency, we create a powerful combination that propels us toward our goals with greater momentum.

One of the most significant benefits of smart hustling efficiency is time management. Time is a finite resource, and once it is spent, we cannot get it back. Smart hustlers understand the value of time and utilize it wisely. They prioritize tasks, focus on high-impact activities, and avoid wasting time on unproductive pursuits. By mastering time management, smart hustlers can accomplish more in a shorter period, providing them with a competitive advantage.

Moreover, efficiency allows us to optimize our use of resources. Whether it is financial, human, or technological resources, smart hustlers allocate them efficiently to achieve maximum returns. This approach minimizes waste, saves costs, and enhances overall productivity. In doing so, they create a sustainable and scalable model for success.

In the realm of business, smart hustling efficiency can make or break a venture. Entrepreneurs who can identify and capitalize on opportunities swiftly gain an edge in the market. They stay ahead of the competition by adapting to changing circumstances and embracing innovation. Additionally, efficient processes within a business lead to higher customer satisfaction and loyalty, fostering a positive reputation and steady growth.

Beyond the business landscape, smart hustling efficiency extends to personal development and well-being. Managing personal goals, relationships, and self-care with efficiency allows individuals to strike a healthy work-life balance.
 By being efficient in their daily routines, they have more time to dedicate to family, hobbies, and self-improvement, leading to greater overall satisfaction and fulfillment.

Cultivating smart hustling efficiency requires self-awareness, continuous learning, and adaptability. Identifying areas where improvement is needed and seeking solutions to streamline processes are crucial steps in this journey. Moreover, staying open to new ideas and being willing to learn from others' experiences can provide valuable insights and shortcuts to success.

However, it is essential to remember that smart hustling efficiency is not about cutting corners or sacrificing quality. Instead, it emphasizes working smarter, not just harder, to achieve our objectives. Maintaining a balance between efficiency and effectiveness ensures that the quality of our work remains top-notch.

In conclusion, understanding the importance of smart hustling efficiency is a transformative mindset that elevates our achievements and impacts various aspects of our lives. By mastering time management, optimizing resource utilization, and embracing innovation, we can create a sustainable path toward success. Whether in the realm of business or personal development, the combination of hustle and efficiency unlocks the true potential of human capability. So, let us embark on this journey together and harness the power of smart hustling efficiency to shape a better future.

# CHAPTER 2

# SETTING CLEAR GOALS

In the pursuit of success, setting clear and well-defined goals is the foundation upon which achievement is built. Goals act as guiding beacons, providing direction and purpose to our actions. Without them, we risk wandering aimlessly and squandering our potential. In this comprehension, we will explore the importance of defining objectives and how to create S.M.A.R.T goals to propel ourselves toward success.

# Defining Your Objectives

Before setting goals, it is crucial to define your objectives clearly. Objectives are the broader intentions and aspirations that drive your desire to achieve something meaningful.

They represent the bigger picture and the ultimate outcome you aim to reach. When setting objectives, it's essential to reflect on your passions, values, and long-term vision. By aligning your goals with your core values and aspirations, you create a sense of purpose that fuels your determination to succeed.

To define your objectives, ask yourself thought-provoking questions:

1. What do I truly want to achieve in my personal life, career, or relationships?

2. How will achieving these objectives contribute to my overall happiness and fulfillment?

3. What impact do I want to make on the world or the people around me?

By answering these questions honestly, you can gain a deeper understanding of your objectives and develop a clear sense of direction.

# Creating S.M.A.R.T Goals for Success

Once you have defined your objectives, the next step is to transform them into actionable goals. This is where the S.M.A.R.T goal-setting framework comes into play. S.M.A.R.T stands for Specific, Measurable, Achievable, Relevant, and Time-bound. By adhering to these principles, you can create goals that are both meaningful and attainable.

1. Specific: Be precise and detailed about what you want to achieve. Instead of a vague goal like "become successful," make it specific, such as "increase my sales revenue by 20% in the next quarter."

2. Measurable: Establish criteria to track your progress and measure success. For example, use metrics like revenue, customers acquired, or hours spent on a particular task.

3. Achievable: Set goals that are challenging yet realistic. Be mindful of your abilities, resources, and time constraints. Setting unattainable goals may lead to disappointment and demotivation.

4. Relevant: Ensure that your goals align with your defined objectives. They should contribute to the bigger picture and help you progress toward your ultimate aspirations.

5. Time-bound: Set a deadline for achieving your goals. This adds a sense of urgency and keeps you focused on completing tasks within a specific timeframe.

By implementing the S.M.A.R.T framework, you break down your objectives into actionable steps, making them more manageable and increasing your chances of success. Moreover, it provides a roadmap that guides your efforts, allowing you to track your progress and make necessary adjustments along the way.

As you embark on your journey of setting clear goals and pursuing success, remember that flexibility and adaptability are essential. Life is full of uncertainties, and circumstances may change, requiring you to recalibrate your goals occasionally. Embrace these changes as opportunities for growth and refinement.

In conclusion, setting clear goals is a fundamental aspect of achieving success. By defining your objectives and adopting the S.M.A.R.T goal-setting framework, you equip yourself with the tools to turn aspirations into reality. With determination, focus, and the willingness to adapt, you can chart a path toward personal and professional fulfillment. So, set your sights high, take action with purpose, and let your clear goals propel you to new heights of success.

# CHAPTER 3

# TIME MANAGEMENT STRATEGIES

In the modern gig economy, side hustles have become increasingly popular, providing individuals with opportunities to pursue their passions, supplement their income, or explore new ventures alongside their primary jobs. However, managing a side hustle alongside other responsibilities can be challenging, making effective time management crucial for success. In this comprehension, we will delve into time management strategies specifically tailored for side hustlers, focusing on identifying time-wasting activities, effective time blocking techniques, and prioritizing tasks for optimal productivity.

# Identifying Time-Wasting Activities

The first step in effective time management is recognizing activities that consume valuable time without adding significant value to our goals. Time-wasting activities can vary from person to person and may include excessive social media usage, unproductive meetings, aimless browsing, or dwelling on unimportant tasks. Identifying these time drainers requires self-awareness and honest evaluation of our daily habits. Once identified, we can take proactive steps to minimize or eliminate them from our routines, allowing us to reclaim precious time for more meaningful and productive endeavors.

For side hustlers, time is a precious and limited resource. To maximize productivity, it is essential to recognize and eliminate time-wasting activities that do not contribute to the growth of the side hustle or the achievement of personal goals. Some common time-wasting activities include excessive social media scrolling, binge-watching TV shows, or engaging in idle conversations. By identifying and reducing these distractions, side hustlers can allocate more time and energy to activities that propel their side projects forward.

For example, Sarah, a side hustler running an online handmade jewelry business, realized that she was spending several hours each day on social media without any clear purpose. After identifying this time-wasting activity, she set specific time limits for social media usage and dedicated more time to designing and promoting her products, resulting in increased sales and business growth.

# Effective Time Blocking Techniques

Time blocking is an invaluable technique for side hustlers to structure their day, ensuring they allocate dedicated time for their side projects amidst their other commitments. Here are some effective time blocking techniques for side hustlers:

a. Flexible Time Blocks: Side hustlers often face fluctuating schedules due to their primary jobs or other responsibilities. Adopting flexible time blocks allows them to adjust their side hustle activities based on their availability. For instance, they could set aside two to three hours on weekdays and longer blocks on weekends to work on their side projects.

b. Combination of Tasks: Side hustlers can combine related tasks within time blocks to enhance efficiency. For example, during a designated time block, they can handle customer inquiries, work on new product designs, and update their website all in one sitting.

c. Buffer Time: Allocating buffer time between time blocks provides a breather and allows for unexpected events or breaks. This flexibility ensures side hustlers can adapt to unforeseen circumstances while maintaining their focus.

Here are some effective time blocking techniques:

a. The Pomodoro Technique: This technique involves breaking work into intervals, usually 25 minutes, followed by a short break. After completing a set of four intervals, take a more extended break. The Pomodoro Technique enhances productivity and prevents burnout.

b. Theme Days: Designate specific days of the week for particular types of tasks. For example, you might have a day dedicated to client meetings, another for creative work, and yet another for administrative tasks. This approach allows you to immerse yourself in similar activities, increasing focus and productivity.

c. Time Blocking by Priority: Prioritize tasks based on urgency and importance, and allocate specific time blocks to work on them. This way, you ensure that essential tasks receive the attention they deserve and avoid procrastination.

# Prioritizing Tasks for Optimal Productivity

With limited time available, effective prioritization is crucial for side hustlers. Prioritizing tasks helps them focus on high-impact activities and ensures that essential tasks are completed on time. Here are some examples of prioritizing tasks for side hustlers:

a. Income-Generating Tasks: Prioritize tasks that directly contribute to generating income from the side hustle. For instance, if a side hustler runs a freelance writing business, they might prioritize completing client projects and sending invoices promptly.

b. Learning and Skill Development: Invest time in learning new skills or improving existing ones related to the side hustle. Side hustlers can allocate time for reading industry-related books, taking online courses, or attending relevant workshops.

c. Networking and Marketing: Building a network and marketing the side hustle are essential for growth. Side hustlers can prioritize activities like attending networking events, engaging on social media, and reaching out to potential collaborators or customers.

For instance, Mark, a software engineer with a passion for photography, started a side hustle offering photography services. He identified networking as a priority and spent time attending photography meetups, connecting with potential clients, and collaborating with local businesses. As a result, his side hustle gained exposure, leading to more bookings and referrals.

In conclusion, effective time management is a crucial factor in the success of side hustlers. By identifying time-wasting activities, adopting effective time blocking techniques, and prioritizing tasks, side hustlers can maximize productivity, achieve their goals, and create a fulfilling balance between their side projects and other responsibilities. As side hustlers embrace these time management strategies, they unlock the full potential of their ventures, taking them one step closer to turning their passions into thriving businesses or meaningful pursuits.

# CHAPTER 4
# LEVERAGING YOUR STRENGTHS

In the pursuit of success and productivity, understanding and leveraging our strengths play a pivotal role. By identifying our core competencies and learning to delegate or outsource non-core tasks, we can focus on what truly matters and optimize our efficiency. Let's delve into the importance of this strategy and explore how it can transform our approach to hustle smart, not hard.

## Identifying Your Core Competencies

Firstly, identifying our core competencies is a fundamental step in the journey of leveraging our strengths. Core competencies are the unique skills, knowledge, and expertise that set us apart from others. These competencies reflect our innate talents and abilities, representing the areas where we can excel and deliver exceptional results. By honing in on these strengths, we can align our pursuits with our natural inclinations, increasing our chances of success.

Recognizing our core competencies requires self-reflection and introspection. We must assess our experiences, achievements, and the activities that ignite passion within us. Seeking feedback from mentors, colleagues, or friends can also offer valuable insights into our strengths. Armed with this knowledge, we gain a clearer understanding of where our focus should lie, and we can align our goals with our areas of expertise.

## Delegating or Outsourcing Non-core Tasks

Once we have identified our core competencies, the next step is to delegate or outsource non-core tasks. No one can excel at everything, and attempting to do so can lead to burnout and diminished results.

Delegating involves entrusting tasks or responsibilities to others who possess the necessary skills, while outsourcing involves seeking external experts or services to handle specific functions.

Delegating non-core tasks allows us to free up valuable time and mental energy to concentrate on what we do best. It fosters a sense of collaboration within a team or organization, as everyone can contribute their unique strengths to achieve collective goals. Moreover, delegating empowers team members by providing them with opportunities to grow and showcase their abilities.

Outsourcing, on the other hand, can be an efficient way to tap into specialized expertise. Whether it is marketing, accounting, or IT support, outsourcing non-core functions to professionals who excel in those areas can lead to higher quality outcomes and cost-effectiveness. It also enables us to focus on strategic decision-making and innovation, leaving routine tasks to experts outside the organization.

However, delegation and outsourcing require effective communication and clear expectations. Properly conveying the desired outcomes, timelines, and performance metrics ensures that the tasks are executed to the best possible standard. Additionally, trust and accountability are essential when delegating or outsourcing, as it involves relying on others to carry out critical responsibilities.

It is crucial to remember that leveraging strengths through delegation and outsourcing is not about avoiding challenges or taking the easy way out. Instead, it is a strategic move that allows us to allocate resources optimally and maximize productivity. By focusing on what we do best and surrounding ourselves with a talented and diverse support network, we build a strong foundation for long-term success.

Furthermore, this approach fosters a growth mindset. By recognizing that we cannot do everything alone, we embrace the power of collaboration and seek opportunities to learn from others. As we expand our network and engage with diverse perspectives, we open ourselves up to new ideas and approaches that can further enhance our performance.

In conclusion, Identifying Core Competencies and Delegating or Outsourcing Non-core Tasks empower us to excel in areas where we have a natural advantage, while also fostering a collaborative and growth-oriented mindset. By streamlining our efforts and focusing on what truly matters, we can achieve greater efficiency, productivity, and success in our personal and professional pursuits.

# CHAPTER 5

# EMBRACING THE POWER OF FOCUS

In a world that constantly demands our attention and tempts us with an abundance of distractions, embracing the power of focus has become more crucial than ever. The concept of "hustling smart, not hard" centers on the idea that efficiency and productivity stem from directing our energy towards the most important tasks with laser-like concentration. This comprehension explores the significance of avoiding multitasking and distractions while developing unwavering focus, leading to enhanced performance and a more fulfilling life.

# Avoiding Multitasking and Distractions

Multitasking has long been considered a badge of productivity, but research has shown that it can be counterproductive and detrimental to our cognitive abilities. The human brain functions optimally when focused on one task at a time. Attempting to juggle multiple tasks simultaneously divides our attention, causing a reduction in overall productivity and an increased likelihood of errors. Embracing the power of focus means resisting the temptation to multitask and dedicating our undivided attention to a single task until completion.

Distractions, both internal and external, pose another challenge to maintaining focus. In today's digitally connected world, notifications, emails, social media, and other interruptions constantly vie for our attention. These distractions not only consume our time but also disrupt our ability to concentrate deeply on important tasks.

Recognizing and minimizing distractions is key to unlocking our full potential and achieving meaningful outcomes.

To avoid multitasking and distractions, it is essential to create an environment conducive to focus. Minimizing external disturbances, such as turning off notifications and finding a quiet workspace, helps cultivate an atmosphere that encourages deep concentration. Additionally, setting clear boundaries with others, both personally and professionally, can help protect our focused time.

# Developing Laser-like Concentration

Developing laser-like concentration requires practice and discipline. Mindfulness techniques, such as meditation and deep breathing exercises, can aid in training the mind to be more present and attentive. Regular exercise, sufficient sleep, and a healthy diet also contribute to mental clarity and focus.

Moreover, time management plays a vital role in embracing the power of focus. Prioritizing tasks based on their importance and urgency allows us to allocate our time efficiently and avoid feeling overwhelmed. Breaking larger tasks into smaller, manageable chunks can make them less daunting and enhance our ability to concentrate on each segment effectively.

In today's fast-paced world, distractions may seem unavoidable. However, by setting boundaries and practicing self-discipline, we can regain control over our focus and productivity.

Embracing the power of focus not only enhances our professional endeavors but also improves our overall well-being and happiness.

Studies have shown that individuals who consistently exhibit laser-like concentration tend to experience higher job satisfaction and lower stress levels. The ability to fully immerse oneself in a task, also known as "flow," leads to a sense of fulfillment and accomplishment.

Embracing the power of focus allows us to make the most of our time, leading to greater efficiency, increased creativity, and improved problem-solving skills.

In conclusion, embracing the power of focus by avoiding multitasking and distractions while developing laser-like concentration is a transformative practice that can significantly impact our personal and professional lives. By dedicating our full attention to each task and setting boundaries with distractions, we can unlock our potential and achieve greater productivity and success.

Developing the habit of focusing smartly allows us to make better use of our time, experience higher levels of fulfillment, and ultimately lead more meaningful and balanced lives. So, let us embrace the art of focusing and take charge of our journey towards a more focused, efficient, and rewarding future.

# CHAPTER 6

# BUILDING A WINNING MINDSET

In the pursuit of success, having a winning mindset is the foundation upon which extraordinary achievements are built. A winning mindset empowers individuals to hustle smart, not just hard, by harnessing their inner strength and conquering self-doubt and limiting beliefs. This powerful mental attitude also enables them to cultivate resilience and persistence, overcoming obstacles that stand in their way.

## Overcoming Self-doubt and Limiting Beliefs

Self-doubt and limiting beliefs can be formidable barriers on the path to success. They manifest as internal voices that question one's abilities, worthiness, and potential for success. These negative thoughts can create a self-imposed glass ceiling, limiting what individuals believe they can achieve. Overcoming these obstacles requires a conscious effort to rewire the mind and develop a positive self-image.

One way to conquer self-doubt is through self-awareness. Recognizing and acknowledging these doubts is the first step toward dismantling their power. By understanding the root causes of these beliefs, individuals can challenge their validity and replace them with empowering affirmations. Building a strong support system of mentors, friends, or coaches who believe in their potential can also help individuals overcome self-doubt and gain the confidence to pursue their goals relentlessly.

In parallel, defeating limiting beliefs involves embracing a growth mindset. This mindset, popularized by psychologist Carol Dweck, emphasizes that abilities and intelligence can be developed through dedication and hard work. Embracing a growth mindset encourages individuals to view challenges as opportunities for growth rather than insurmountable roadblocks. This shift in perspective fosters a willingness to learn, adapt, and continually improve, leading to greater success in the long run.

## Cultivating Resilience and Persistence

Cultivating resilience and persistence is another essential aspect of a winning mindset. In the journey to achieve ambitious goals, setbacks and failures are inevitable. Resilience empowers individuals to bounce back from adversity, learn from their experiences, and emerge stronger than before. It is the ability to keep moving forward, even in the face of disappointment or obstacles.

Developing resilience requires reframing failures as opportunities for learning and growth. Rather than seeing failure as a sign of incompetence, a resilient individual sees it as a stepping stone to success. They analyze what went wrong, identify lessons learned, and use that knowledge to refine their strategies.

This adaptive mindset allows them to persist in the face of challenges, knowing that success often comes after numerous attempts.

Furthermore, surrounding oneself with a supportive network of like-minded individuals can significantly contribute to cultivating resilience and persistence. Sharing experiences with others who have faced similar challenges can provide encouragement and inspiration. Moreover, having a support system to lean on during difficult times can help individuals stay focused and motivated, enhancing their chances of success.

In addition to resilience, persistence is the unwavering commitment to achieving one's goals, regardless of setbacks or obstacles. A persistent individual maintains their focus and determination, even when the going gets tough.

They view temporary failures as stepping stones and remain undeterred in their pursuit of success.

Building a winning mindset that encompasses overcoming self-doubt and limiting beliefs, as well as cultivating resilience and persistence, is a transformative process that requires dedication and perseverance. It involves continuous self-reflection, learning, and adaptability. By taking deliberate steps to develop this mindset, individuals can unleash their full potential and become unstoppable forces in their pursuit of success.

In conclusion, hustling smart, not just hard, begins with cultivating a winning mindset. Overcoming self-doubt and limiting beliefs is the first step in unleashing one's true capabilities. Embracing a growth mindset and seeking support from mentors and peers can empower individuals to conquer their doubts and embrace their potential for growth. Additionally, developing resilience and persistence enables them to navigate challenges with grace, emerging stronger and more determined to achieve their goals. As individuals build and nurture their winning mindset, they embark on a journey of personal transformation, unlocking their limitless potential for success and fulfillment.

# CHAPTER 7

# CREATING SYSTEMS AND WORKFLOWS

In the pursuit of hustling smart, not just hard, creating effective systems and workflows is paramount to achieving optimal efficiency and productivity. Systems and workflows provide a structured approach to tasks, streamlining processes and minimizing wasted time and effort. Additionally, leveraging automation and productivity tools further enhances the efficiency of these systems, allowing individuals to focus on high-impact activities and maximize their results.

## Streamlining Processes for Efficiency

Streamlining processes for efficiency involves designing systematic and well-defined approaches to common tasks. It begins with a thorough analysis of the entire workflow, identifying bottlenecks and areas where improvements can be made. By breaking down complex processes into smaller, manageable steps, individuals can optimize each stage for maximum efficiency.

To build efficient systems, it is crucial to establish clear roles and responsibilities. Delegating tasks based on team members' strengths ensures that each aspect of the workflow is handled by the most suitable individual. Moreover, providing proper training and resources to team members enhances their capabilities, contributing to overall process efficiency.

The continuous improvement mindset is also integral to streamlining processes. By regularly evaluating the effectiveness of systems and workflows, individuals can identify areas for enhancement and implement iterative changes. This approach fosters a culture of adaptability and optimization, ensuring that the systems in place remain relevant and effective over time.

## Automation and Productivity Tools

Automation plays a significant role in optimizing efficiency and minimizing manual intervention. By automating repetitive and time-consuming tasks, individuals free up valuable time and resources to focus on more strategic and creative endeavors. Automation can be achieved through various tools and software, such as customer relationship management

(CRM) systems, project management tools, and email marketing platforms.

Moreover, automation eliminates the risk of human errors, enhancing accuracy and consistency in tasks. This, in turn, leads to improved quality and higher levels of customer satisfaction.
For instance, automated email sequences can ensure timely and personalized communications with clients, strengthening relationships and driving business growth.

Productivity tools are another essential aspect of hustling smart. These tools encompass a wide range of applications and software that aid in organizing, managing, and executing tasks efficiently.

Project management tools like Trello and Asana help individuals track project progress, assign tasks, and collaborate with team members seamlessly. Note-taking and organization apps like Evernote enable quick access to essential information and ideas.

Furthermore, time-tracking and task management tools help individuals stay focused and accountable. By monitoring how time is allocated to various activities, individuals can identify areas where productivity can be improved and implement adjustments accordingly.

While automation and productivity tools can significantly enhance efficiency, it is essential to strike a balance between automation and personalization. Human touch and personalized interactions remain invaluable in fostering strong relationships with customers and team members.

Therefore, individuals should carefully choose the aspects of their workflows to automate, ensuring that human interaction is still prioritized when it matters most.

In conclusion, creating systems and workflows is a fundamental aspect of hustling smart, not just hard. Streamlining processes for efficiency ensures that tasks are executed in the most optimized and productive manner.

By embracing automation and productivity tools, individuals can further enhance their efficiency, freeing up time and resources for high-impact activities.

However, it is essential to maintain a human touch and adaptability within these systems to foster meaningful relationships and ongoing improvement. Through a deliberate and thoughtful approach to creating systems and leveraging technology, individuals can elevate their productivity and achieve remarkable success in their endeavors.

# CHAPTER 8

# THE ART OF NEGOTIATION

The art of negotiation is a crucial skill that can make a significant difference in achieving favorable outcomes. Negotiation involves a strategic and collaborative process of reaching agreements, and mastering this art allows individuals to navigate various situations with confidence and finesse. By understanding effective negotiation strategies and aiming for win-win deals, negotiators can secure their interests while building long-lasting and mutually beneficial relationships.

# Strategies for Successful Negotiations

Successful negotiations start with preparation. Before entering any negotiation, it is essential to conduct thorough research on the subject matter, the parties involved, and potential alternatives. Knowing the interests, needs, and constraints of both sides empowers negotiators to make informed decisions and develop creative solutions. By having a clear understanding of their own objectives and boundaries, negotiators can strategize effectively and stay composed during the negotiation process.

Listening attentively is a fundamental aspect of effective negotiation. Understanding the other party's perspective and concerns allows negotiators to identify common ground and areas of potential agreement. Active listening shows respect and builds trust, fostering a positive atmosphere for open communication.

Communication skills play a pivotal role in negotiations. Expressing ideas clearly and concisely, while being receptive to the other party's viewpoints, enhances the negotiation process. Using persuasive language and presenting compelling arguments can influence the other party to consider the proposed solutions more favorably.

Emotional intelligence is another critical element in successful negotiations. Recognizing and managing emotions, both in oneself and others, can prevent the negotiation from becoming confrontational or hostile. Remaining composed and empathetic, even in challenging situations, strengthens the chances of finding common ground and reaching satisfactory agreements.

Aim for a win-win approach in negotiations, seeking mutually beneficial outcomes for all parties involved. By reframing the negotiation as a collaborative problem-solving exercise, negotiators foster a spirit of cooperation rather than competition. This approach promotes trust and goodwill, paving the way for enduring partnerships.

# Negotiating Win-Win Deals

Negotiating win-win deals involves being creative and flexible. Exploring different options and proposing alternative solutions can lead to outcomes that satisfy the interests of both parties. By focusing on shared goals and emphasizing the benefits of collaboration, negotiators can build strong foundations for successful and long-term business relationships.

However, it is crucial to know when to walk away from a negotiation that is not yielding favorable results. Setting clear boundaries and knowing one's "best alternative to a negotiated agreement" (BATNA) allows negotiators to gauge the value of the deal they are pursuing. If the negotiated terms do not meet or exceed the BATNA, it may be more advantageous to walk away and explore other opportunities.

Furthermore, negotiators should be mindful of ethical considerations throughout the negotiation process.

Maintaining honesty, integrity, and transparency in all dealings builds trust and credibility. Trust is a valuable asset in any negotiation, as it enables parties to collaborate confidently and achieve mutually beneficial outcomes.

Win-win deals, also known as mutual gain or integrative negotiations, are negotiation outcomes in which both parties involved benefit and achieve their objectives. Unlike win-lose scenarios, where one party's gain comes at the expense of the other, win-win deals emphasize collaboration and problem-solving to find solutions that meet the needs and interests of all parties. These agreements foster positive and sustainable relationships, as both sides are satisfied with the outcomes and feel valued in the negotiation process.

**Key Principles of Win-Win Deals:**

1. Collaboration: Win-win deals focus on cooperation and collaboration between parties. Rather than viewing negotiation as a zero-sum game, where one party's gain equals the other's loss, negotiators work together to identify common interests and find creative solutions that satisfy both sides.

2. Interests over Positions: Instead of fixating on specific demands or positions, negotiators in win-win deals concentrate on underlying interests and motivations. By understanding each party's underlying needs, desires, and constraints, negotiators can generate options that address these interests and create value for all involved.

3. Value Creation: Win-win negotiations prioritize value creation for all parties. Negotiators seek to expand the pie and find opportunities for mutual gain. This approach contrasts with distributive negotiations, where the focus is on dividing a fixed pie, often leading to a more competitive and confrontational dynamic.

4. Long-Term Perspective: Win-win deals are conducive to building enduring and trusting relationships. By prioritizing mutual benefits and maintaining a collaborative spirit, parties can establish a foundation for future cooperation and future negotiations.

5. Flexibility and Creativity: Negotiators in win-win deals are open to exploring various options and considering creative solutions. Being flexible in their approach enables them to uncover alternatives that meet the interests of both parties and, in some cases, exceed initial expectations.

**Benefits of Win-Win Deals:**

1. Improved Relationships: Win-win deals foster positive and cooperative relationships between parties. This leads to enhanced trust, mutual respect, and a willingness to work together on future opportunities.

2. Higher Satisfaction: Both parties leave the negotiation feeling satisfied with the agreement,

as their interests have been adequately addressed. This satisfaction contributes to a positive perception of the negotiation process and the other party involved.

3. Increased Value: Win-win deals often create additional value beyond the initial objectives of both parties.
By focusing on collaboration and creative solutions, negotiators can generate outcomes that are superior to what either party could have achieved individually.

4. Lower Risk of Disputes: The cooperative and constructive nature of win-win deals reduces the likelihood of future disputes or conflicts. Parties are more likely to uphold their commitments and maintain a cooperative spirit in the long run.

5. Positive Reputation: Consistently pursuing win-win deals can enhance an individual's or organization's reputation as a fair and

collaborative negotiator. This reputation can attract more opportunities and partners willing to engage in productive negotiations.

Win-win deals are the hallmark of successful negotiations in which both parties find satisfaction and achieve their objectives. By prioritizing collaboration, identifying interests, and seeking creative solutions, negotiators can build positive and enduring relationships while maximizing the value created in the negotiation process.

Win-win deals embody the essence of hustling smart, as they lead to mutually beneficial outcomes and lay the foundation for continued success in future ventures.

# Emotional Intelligence in Negotiation

Emotional intelligence (EI) plays a significant role in negotiation, as it encompasses the ability to understand and manage emotions effectively, both in oneself and others. In the context of negotiation, emotional intelligence is a crucial skill that can influence the outcomes of the negotiation process and shape the dynamics between parties.

Key Aspects of Emotional Intelligence in Negotiation:

1. Self-Awareness: Self-aware negotiators recognize their own emotions and how those emotions might impact their decision-making and communication during the negotiation.
By being aware of their emotional state, negotiators can better manage their reactions and responses, ensuring that their emotions do not cloud their judgment or lead to impulsive decisions.

2. Emotional Regulation: Emotionally intelligent negotiators can effectively manage and regulate their emotions during the negotiation process. They remain composed and focused even in tense or high-pressure situations, allowing them to think clearly and make rational decisions. Emotional regulation prevents emotional outbursts that could derail

the negotiation or damage the relationship with the other party.

3. Empathy: Empathy is a critical aspect of emotional intelligence in negotiation. Empathetic negotiators can understand and appreciate the emotions and perspectives of the other party. By putting themselves in the shoes of the other negotiator, they can gain valuable insights into their interests, needs, and concerns, which can help in finding mutually beneficial solutions.

4. Active Listening: Emotionally intelligent negotiators are skilled active listeners. They pay close attention to what the other party is saying and listen not only to the words but also to the emotions and underlying interests being expressed.
Active listening fosters better understanding and shows respect for the other party's viewpoint.

5. Social Skills: Effective negotiation involves building rapport and establishing a positive relationship with the other party. Emotionally intelligent negotiators possess strong social

skills that enable them to communicate effectively, build trust, and engage in constructive dialogue. These social skills contribute to a cooperative and collaborative negotiation environment.

Benefits of Emotional Intelligence in Negotiation:

1. Building Rapport: Emotionally intelligent negotiators can establish rapport with the other party, creating a foundation of trust and goodwill.
Building rapport improves communication and enhances the likelihood of reaching mutually beneficial agreements.

2. Conflict Resolution: Emotional intelligence enables negotiators to manage conflicts effectively. They can de-escalate tense situations, address emotions constructively, and focus on finding common ground for resolution.

3. Negotiation Flexibility: Emotionally intelligent negotiators can adapt their approach to suit the emotional dynamics of the

negotiation. They can remain open to various perspectives and engage in a flexible negotiation style that encourages collaboration.

4. Enhanced Communication: Emotional intelligence improves communication skills, allowing negotiators to articulate their interests clearly and listen attentively to the other party's concerns. Effective communication facilitates the exchange of information and facilitates problem-solving.

5. Preserving Relationships: Successful negotiation is not just about reaching an agreement; it's also about maintaining positive relationships for future interactions.
Emotional intelligence helps negotiators navigate difficult discussions while preserving the relationship with the other party.

In conclusion, the art of negotiation is a foundational skill in the world of hustling smart, not just hard. By employing effective negotiation strategies, individuals can navigate complex situations with finesse and achieve successful outcomes.

Prioritizing win-win deals fosters collaboration and builds lasting relationships, which are vital in the pursuit of sustained success. By being prepared, actively listening, and practicing emotional intelligence, negotiators can navigate challenges and secure their interests while promoting positive and productive interactions.

Striving for ethical and respectful negotiations not only strengthens the negotiation process but also enhances the overall reputation and credibility of the parties involved. Ultimately, the art of negotiation empowers individuals to navigate the complexities of business and life with confidence, creating opportunities for growth, prosperity, and meaningful connections.

# CHAPTER 9

# NETWORKING AND RELATIONSHIP BUILDING

In the realm of hustling smart, the art of networking and relationship building holds immense significance. Building meaningful connections and leveraging your network can be transformative in unlocking opportunities, fostering personal growth, and achieving success.

# Building Meaningful Connections

Building meaningful connections is more than just exchanging business cards or connecting on social media. It involves cultivating genuine relationships based on mutual respect, trust, and shared values. These connections can be with peers, mentors, industry experts, clients, or collaborators. By investing time and effort into nurturing these relationships, individuals can create a network that offers both personal and professional support.

To build meaningful connections, individuals must approach networking with authenticity. Genuine interest in others' experiences and perspectives lays the foundation for fruitful relationships. Active listening and empathy foster connections on a deeper level, creating a sense of trust and rapport.

Attending industry events, conferences, and workshops provides valuable opportunities to meet like-minded individuals and potential collaborators.
However, the value of networking extends beyond formal events. Engaging in online communities, forums, and social media platforms relevant to one's field also offers avenues for building connections and sharing insights.

One of the key aspects of building meaningful connections is active listening. Taking the time to understand others' perspectives and interests not only demonstrates empathy but also helps in finding common ground. Meaningful connections are forged when individuals feel heard and valued. Consistency is also vital – staying in touch, checking in, and offering assistance when needed contribute to the growth of authentic relationships.

# Leveraging Your Network for Opportunities

Once a network is established, leveraging it for opportunities becomes a strategic endeavor. The network acts as a reservoir of knowledge, connections, and expertise that can be tapped into when seeking advice, partnerships, or even career advancements. For instance, seeking mentorship from experienced professionals within the network can provide valuable guidance and insights into navigating challenges.

Leveraging your network for opportunities goes beyond seeking immediate gains. It's about tapping into the collective knowledge, experiences, and resources that your network possesses. Opportunities often arise from unexpected places, and a well-nurtured network can provide insights, referrals, and collaborations that propel your journey toward success.

Moreover, leveraging a network for opportunities often involves reciprocity. By actively contributing to the network's growth and success, individuals reinforce their relationships and enhance their reputation within the community. Sharing knowledge, offering assistance, and connecting others within the network not only strengthens existing connections but also attracts new ones.

In the professional world, opportunities often arise through referrals and recommendations. A strong network can serve as a platform for receiving and providing such referrals, expanding one's reach and access to potential clients, partners, or employers.
This interconnected web of relationships creates a multiplier effect, where opportunities cascade through the network.

Networking and relationship building extend beyond immediate professional gains. They can also foster personal growth and development. Exposure to diverse perspectives and experiences within a network enhances one's understanding of various industries, cultures, and viewpoints. This broader perspective contributes to well-rounded decision-making and creativity.

However, it is essential to approach networking and relationship building with genuine intentions rather than solely focusing on personal gains. Authenticity and a willingness to contribute without immediate expectations of return build a strong foundation for lasting connections and opportunities.

Moreover, networking transcends traditional in-person events. Online platforms, social media, and virtual communities have expanded the scope of networking, making it easier to connect with people from around the world. Engaging in thoughtful discussions, contributing to relevant online forums, and participating in webinars or virtual conferences can help you expand your network and learn from a diverse range of individuals.

In conclusion, networking and relationship building are essential components of hustling smart. Building meaningful connections involves genuine interactions and active listening, leading to valuable relationships that provide both personal and professional support. Leveraging your network for opportunities involves reciprocity, offering assistance, and sharing resources. By nurturing relationships and contributing to your network, you create a supportive community that enhances your personal growth and opens doors to various opportunities on your path to success.

# CHAPTER 10

# MARKETING SMARTER, NOT HARDER

In the dynamic and competitive landscape of modern business, the concept of marketing smarter, not harder, has emerged as a guiding principle for achieving impactful results with efficiency and precision. This approach focuses on employing targeted marketing strategies and maximizing the return on investment (ROI) of marketing efforts, ultimately leading to a more effective and successful marketing campaign. By focusing resources on the right audience and optimizing strategies, businesses can achieve better outcomes while conserving valuable resources.

# Targeted Marketing Strategies

Targeted marketing strategies lie at the heart of marketing smarter. Instead of casting a wide net in the hope of reaching a broad audience, targeted marketing involves tailoring campaigns to specific segments of the market that are most likely to engage and convert. This approach acknowledges that not all consumers are the same and that delivering personalized and relevant content to a well-defined audience is far more effective.

Targeted marketing strategies form the cornerstone of this approach. Instead of adopting a one-size-fits-all approach, businesses identify specific segments of their audience that are most likely to resonate with their products or services. This allows for a more personalized and relevant communication that captures the attention of potential customers.

Understanding the demographics, behaviors, and preferences of the target audience is critical. This information enables businesses to craft tailored marketing messages that address the unique needs and pain points of their ideal customers. By aligning marketing efforts with the interests of the audience, businesses can establish a deeper connection and increase the likelihood of conversion.

Moreover, targeted marketing strategies extend beyond demographics. Psychographics, such as values, beliefs, and lifestyle preferences, play a significant role in shaping consumer behavior. By tapping into these psychological factors, businesses can create campaigns that resonate on a more emotional level, forging stronger brand loyalty and customer relationships.

The foundation of targeted marketing is market segmentation, where the market is divided into distinct groups based on shared characteristics, behaviors, or preferences. This segmentation allows marketers to create tailored messages that resonate with each group, increasing the likelihood of capturing their attention and driving desired actions.

By understanding the unique needs and motivations of these segments, marketers can craft compelling narratives that speak directly to them.

Moreover, targeted marketing strategies encompass various channels and mediums that are most relevant to the chosen audience. This could involve leveraging social media platforms, email marketing, content marketing, or even experiential events. By selecting the right channels, marketers ensure that their message reaches their target audience where they are most likely to engage.

# Maximizing ROI on Marketing Efforts

Maximizing ROI on marketing efforts is the natural outcome of implementing targeted strategies. ROI measures the effectiveness of a marketing campaign by comparing the gains achieved against the costs incurred. To enhance ROI, marketers must adopt a data-driven approach that enables them to track and measure the success of their campaigns accurately.

One of the key components of maximizing ROI is setting clear and measurable objectives for each marketing initiative. Whether it's lead generation, brand awareness, or sales conversion, having specific goals allows marketers to assess the impact of their efforts accurately. With these goals in place, marketers can monitor key performance indicators (KPIs) and adjust their strategies in real time based on the data collected.

A key aspect of maximizing ROI is continuous optimization. By regularly reviewing campaign performance and making data-driven adjustments, businesses can refine their strategies for better results. This iterative process allows for quick adaptation to changing market trends and customer preferences.

Investing in digital marketing channels can significantly enhance the ROI on marketing efforts. Digital platforms provide tools for precise targeting, allowing businesses to reach the right audience with minimal wastage.

Social media advertising, search engine optimization (SEO), and pay-per-click (PPC) advertising are examples of digital strategies that can yield high returns when executed strategically.

In addition to digital channels, content marketing is another avenue for maximizing ROI. Creating valuable and relevant content not only engages the audience but also positions the business as an authority in their industry.

This organic approach can yield long-term benefits by attracting and retaining customers through informative and valuable content.

Collaboration and partnerships also contribute to maximizing ROI. Strategic alliances with complementary businesses can expand the reach of marketing efforts and tap into new audiences. Joint promotions, co-hosted events, and cross-promotions can all amplify the impact of marketing campaigns while sharing the associated costs.

Furthermore, the use of analytics and marketing technology plays a crucial role in optimizing ROI. Advanced analytics tools provide insights into consumer behavior, preferences, and engagement patterns. By analyzing this data, marketers can fine-tune their strategies, allocate resources more effectively, and make informed decisions that lead to higher ROI.

Automation also plays a significant role in maximizing ROI. Marketing automation platforms enable the execution of repetitive tasks, such as sending follow-up emails or segmenting audiences, without manual intervention. This not only saves time and resources but also ensures consistent and timely communication with prospects and customers.

In conclusion, marketing smarter, not harder, is a strategic approach that focuses on targeted marketing strategies and maximizing ROI on marketing efforts. By tailoring campaigns to specific segments of the market and leveraging data-driven insights, marketers can create more relevant and engaging content that resonates with their audience. The result is a higher likelihood of conversions and customer engagement.

Moreover, by setting clear objectives, utilizing analytics, and embracing automation, marketers can optimize their ROI and ensure that every marketing dollar is well spent. In an era where precision and efficiency are paramount, adopting these principles is a critical step toward achieving marketing success.

# CHAPTER 11

# PRICING FOR PROFITABILITY

In the realm of business, pricing strategies play a pivotal role in determining profitability and long-term sustainability. Effectively pricing products or services requires a deep understanding of cost structures and the art of setting competitive yet profitable prices. Balancing these elements is essential to maximize revenue while ensuring the business remains financially viable and competitive in the market.

# Understanding Cost Structures

Understanding cost structures is the foundation of successful pricing. This involves a comprehensive analysis of all expenses associated with producing and delivering a product or service. These costs encompass both direct costs, such as raw materials and labor, and indirect costs like overhead expenses and marketing. A thorough understanding of cost structures empowers businesses to accurately calculate their breakeven point—the minimum sales volume required to cover all costs.

Businesses must have a clear grasp of all the costs associated with producing, marketing, and delivering their products or services. These costs can be categorized as direct costs (such as raw materials and labor) and indirect costs (like overhead and administrative expenses). By accurately accounting for these costs, businesses can determine the minimum price required to cover expenses and avoid operating at a loss.

Furthermore, distinguishing between fixed and variable costs is essential. Fixed costs remain constant regardless of production levels, while variable costs fluctuate based on production volume. This differentiation aids businesses in making informed decisions about pricing adjustments in response to changes in demand or market conditions.

Moreover, different pricing models can be employed based on cost structures. Cost-plus pricing involves adding a predetermined profit margin to the total cost of production. This approach guarantees that each sale contributes to covering costs and generating profit. Value-based pricing, on the other hand, focuses on the perceived value of the product or service to the customer. Businesses adopting this model price their offerings based on the benefits and solutions they provide to the customer, rather than simply covering costs.

# Setting Competitive yet Profitable Prices

Once cost structures are understood, the challenge lies in setting prices that strike a balance between competitiveness and profitability. Pricing too low may attract customers but erode profits, while pricing too high may deter potential buyers. A holistic approach is needed to find the sweet spot.

Setting competitive yet profitable prices requires a delicate balance between attracting customers and ensuring healthy profit margins. While it can be tempting to engage in price wars to capture market share, excessively low prices can erode profitability and compromise the sustainability of the business. Therefore, pricing decisions should be grounded in a comprehensive understanding of the market, competitors, and the unique value proposition the business offers.

Market research is a crucial component of setting competitive prices. Analyzing competitors' pricing strategies and understanding customer behavior provides insights into pricing thresholds and customer expectations. By positioning the product or service appropriately within the market landscape, businesses can command prices that reflect their value while remaining attractive to potential customers.

Furthermore, pricing psychology plays a significant role in influencing consumer perceptions. Strategies such as charm pricing (using prices ending in 9 or 99) and tiered pricing (offering different price levels with varying features) can impact how customers perceive the value of a product or service. Leveraging these psychological pricing techniques can contribute to setting prices that not only cover costs but also entice customers to make a purchase.

Moreover, considering elasticity of demand is crucial. Elastic demand implies that price changes significantly affect demand, while inelastic demand indicates that changes in price have minimal impact. By recognizing demand elasticity, businesses can strategically adjust prices to maximize revenue without alienating customers.

Dynamic pricing, another strategy, involves adjusting prices in real-time based on factors like demand, time of day, or inventory levels. This approach allows businesses to capture additional value during peak periods while offering discounts during off-peak times, thereby optimizing revenue and satisfying different customer segments.

Value-based pricing is yet another technique that ties pricing to the perceived value customers receive. This approach focuses on the benefits and outcomes customers gain from a product or service, rather than just the cost of production. Effective communication of these value propositions can justify higher prices and increase customer willingness to pay.

It is important to note that pricing is not a static endeavor; it requires continuous monitoring and adjustment.

Businesses should regularly assess their pricing strategies based on changes in costs, market conditions, and customer preferences. Dynamic pricing, which involves adjusting prices in real-time based on demand and supply fluctuations, can be particularly effective in industries with rapidly changing conditions.

In conclusion, pricing for profitability is a multifaceted process that involves understanding cost structures and skillfully setting competitive yet profitable prices. By analyzing cost components and choosing appropriate pricing models, businesses can ensure that their offerings cover costs and generate sustainable profits.

Strategic pricing, informed by market research and pricing psychology, positions businesses for success by capturing the right customer segments and maximizing revenue. Ultimately, the art of pricing for profitability is a dynamic and ongoing practice that is central to the financial health and longevity of any business.

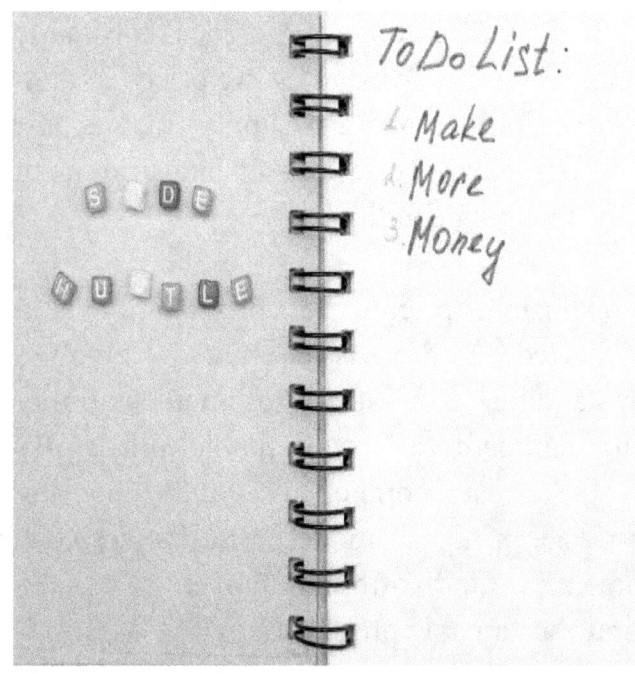

# CHAPTER 12
# FINANCIAL MANAGEMENT AND BUDGETING

In the realm of hustling smart, mastering financial management and budgeting is a critical skill that can make the difference between success and stagnation. Effective budgeting practices and the ability to track financial performance empower individuals to make informed decisions, allocate resources wisely, and achieve their financial goals with precision.

# Effective Budgeting Practices

Effective budgeting practices lay the foundation for sound financial management. A budget serves as a roadmap for allocating funds to various expenses and investments, ensuring that resources are utilized optimally.

It begins with a thorough assessment of income sources and an understanding of fixed and variable expenses. By categorizing and prioritizing expenses, individuals gain clarity on where their money is going and can identify areas for potential savings.

Creating a budget requires setting clear financial goals. Whether it's saving for a major purchase, paying off debt, or building an emergency fund, well-defined goals provide motivation and direction. Budgets should be realistic and flexible, allowing room for unexpected expenses while guiding individuals toward their objectives.

To develop an effective budget:

1. Assess Income and Expenses: Start by thoroughly evaluating sources of income and categorizing expenses. This includes fixed costs (e.g., rent, utilities) and variable expenses (e.g., entertainment, dining out).

2. Set Realistic Goals: Define short-term and long-term financial goals, such as paying off debt, saving for a vacation, or building an emergency fund.

3. Prioritize and Allocate Funds: Assign funds to each category based on priority. Allocate more resources to essential expenses and savings goals while identifying areas where spending can be reduced.

4. Monitor and Adjust: Regularly review your budget to ensure you are staying on track. Make adjustments as needed to accommodate changes in income or unexpected expenses.

5. Avoid Lifestyle Inflation: As income increases, resist the temptation to increase spending proportionally. Instead, prioritize

saving and investing for long-term financial security.

# Tracking Financial Performance

Tracking financial performance is essential to ensure that budgeting efforts are aligned with actual outcomes. Regularly monitoring income and expenses helps individuals identify trends, make necessary adjustments, and stay on track to achieve their financial goals.

This process involves comparing actual expenditures to the budgeted amounts and analyzing any discrepancies.

Technology plays a crucial role in tracking financial performance. Digital tools and apps, such as spreadsheets and financial management apps, allow for real-time tracking and reporting. These tools provide insights into spending patterns, enabling individuals to make timely adjustments to their budgeting strategies.

One effective method of budget tracking is the envelope system, where cash is allocated to specific categories and placed in physical envelopes. Once the envelope is empty, spending in that category stops until the next budgeting period. This method promotes conscious spending and prevents overspending in any given category.

Additionally, understanding cash flow is essential for effective financial management. Cash flow represents the movement of money into and out of an individual's accounts. Positive cash flow indicates that more money is coming in than going out, allowing for savings and investments. Negative cash flow, on the other hand, requires a reevaluation of spending habits and financial priorities.

Financial ratios are also valuable tools for tracking financial performance. Ratios such as the debt-to-income ratio and the savings ratio provide insights into an individual's financial health. They help identify areas that may require attention, such as high levels of debt or insufficient savings.

Moreover, periodic financial reviews are crucial for refining budgeting strategies and long-term planning. These reviews involve analyzing financial goals, progress, and any changes in circumstances that may affect budgeting decisions. Regular reviews ensure that the budget remains aligned with evolving financial objectives.

Review bank statements, credit card statements, and receipts to reconcile expenses and ensure accuracy in your financial tracking.

Look for trends in your spending habits over time. Identify areas where you consistently overspend and find ways to address these patterns.

Regularly assess your progress toward savings and debt reduction goals. Celebrate milestones and make adjustments if progress is slower than anticipated.

Maintain an emergency fund to cover unexpected expenses, helping you avoid derailing your budget when unforeseen circumstances arise.

In conclusion, financial management and budgeting are integral components of hustling smart. Effective budgeting practices guide individuals in allocating resources wisely and achieving their financial goals. Tracking financial performance through technology, methods like the envelope system, and understanding cash flow ensures that budgeting efforts translate into tangible results. By embracing these practices and consistently reviewing their financial strategies, individuals can navigate their financial journey with confidence, achieving stability and success.

# CHAPTER 13

# BALANCING WORK AND LIFE

In a world characterized by constant connectivity and demanding work schedules, finding the delicate balance between work and personal life has become more critical than ever. Achieving work-life harmony is not only essential for maintaining one's well-being but also for optimizing productivity and overall satisfaction. Simultaneously, avoiding burnout and managing stress are vital components of this balance, ensuring that individuals can thrive in both their professional and personal spheres.

# Achieving Work-Life Harmony

Work-life harmony refers to the art of seamlessly integrating work commitments with personal pursuits in a way that allows individuals to excel in both domains without feeling overwhelmed. Unlike the concept of "work-life balance," which implies a rigid separation of work and personal life, work-life harmony acknowledges that these two aspects can coexist and complement each other. It involves setting clear boundaries, prioritizing tasks, and making intentional choices to align work commitments with personal values and goals.

To achieve work-life harmony, it's essential to establish healthy boundaries. This means defining specific work hours and nonnegotiable personal time. During work hours, focus and productivity are paramount, while personal time should be dedicated to rejuvenation and relaxation.

Communicating these boundaries to colleagues, family, and friends helps set expectations and encourages respect for personal time.

Flexibility also plays a crucial role in work-life harmony. With the rise of remote work and flexible schedules, individuals can tailor their work hours to accommodate personal responsibilities. Embracing this flexibility allows for better management of both work and life commitments, contributing to a sense of control and reduced stress.

# Avoiding Burnout and Stress

Avoiding burnout and managing stress are vital aspects of maintaining work-life harmony. Burnout occurs when prolonged periods of stress lead to emotional exhaustion, decreased performance, and a feeling of detachment from work. To prevent burnout, it's essential to recognize the signs of excessive stress and take proactive steps to manage it.

Regular self-care routines are instrumental in managing stress and preventing burnout. Engaging in activities that promote relaxation, such as exercise, mindfulness, hobbies, and spending quality time with loved ones, can alleviate stress and restore mental well-being. Prioritizing sleep, maintaining a balanced diet, and taking breaks during the workday are equally important for maintaining energy levels and preventing burnout.

Additionally, setting realistic expectations and learning to say "no" when necessary are essential tools for avoiding burnout. Accepting that perfection is not always attainable and seeking support when overwhelmed can help individuals manage their workloads effectively and reduce stress.

In conclusion, achieving work-life harmony and preventing burnout are interconnected goals that contribute to an individual's overall well-being and success. By setting boundaries, prioritizing tasks, and embracing flexibility, individuals can create a harmonious integration of work and personal life. Engaging in self-care routines and managing stress proactively are vital components of this balance.

Ultimately, striking a balance between work and life enables individuals to excel in their professional pursuits while maintaining their mental, emotional, and physical health. It empowers them to lead fulfilling lives that encompass meaningful achievements and personal fulfillment.

CHAPTER 14

THE ART OF CONTINUOUS IMPROVEMENT

The pursuit of excellence and lasting success is intricately tied to the art of continuous improvement. This mindset involves a commitment to growth, a willingness to learn from failures, and a dedication to innovative thinking. Embracing continuous improvement not only fosters personal and professional growth but also lays the foundation for sustainable success in an ever-evolving world.

# Cultivating a Growth Mindset

Cultivating a growth mindset is at the core of the art of continuous improvement. This mindset, popularized by psychologist Carol Dweck, is centered around the belief that abilities and intelligence can be developed through effort, dedication, and learning. Those with a growth mindset view challenges as opportunities for growth and believe that failures are stepping stones to success.

Individuals with a growth mindset seek out challenges, persevere in the face of setbacks, and actively seek opportunities to expand their knowledge and skills. They understand that failure is not a reflection of their worth but rather a chance to learn, adapt, and improve. This mindset enables them to remain resilient and open-minded, embracing change as a catalyst for growth.

# Learning from Failures and Mistakes

Learning from failures and mistakes is another cornerstone of continuous improvement. Instead of fearing failure, individuals who prioritize continuous improvement embrace it as a valuable teacher. Analyzing what went wrong, identifying areas for improvement, and implementing changes based on these lessons are crucial steps in the journey of growth.

Moreover, fostering a culture that encourages learning from mistakes is essential in both personal and professional spheres. Emphasizing open communication, constructive feedback, and a non-judgmental approach to failures creates an environment where individuals are more likely to take calculated risks and innovate.

# Innovating for Sustainable Success

Innovation is the third pillar of continuous improvement. The ability to think creatively, challenge the status quo, and explore new solutions is vital for staying ahead in an ever-changing world. Innovation is not limited to groundbreaking discoveries; it can also involve incremental improvements that enhance efficiency, quality, and customer satisfaction.

To foster innovation, individuals must be open to diverse perspectives and willing to step out of their comfort zones. Encouraging collaboration and cross-functional thinking can spark new ideas and approaches. Organizations that prioritize innovation often dedicate resources to research and development, empower employees to experiment, and create an environment where calculated risks are welcomed.

Furthermore, sustaining success through continuous improvement involves embracing a long-term perspective. It's not about seeking quick fixes but rather about consistently fine-tuning strategies and approaches to remain relevant and competitive. The art of continuous improvement acknowledges that success is not a destination but a dynamic journey.

In conclusion, the art of continuous improvement is a mindset that encompasses cultivating a growth mindset, learning from failures and mistakes, and embracing innovation. It is a commitment to ongoing learning, growth, and adaptation in the pursuit of personal and professional excellence. By nurturing this mindset, individuals and organizations can lay the foundation for sustainable success in a rapidly changing world.

# CHAPTER 15

# EMBRACING CHANGE AND ADAPTABILITY

In a world characterized by constant evolution and unforeseen shifts, the ability to embrace change and adapt with agility has become a hallmark of success. This mindset enables individuals and organizations to not only survive but thrive in a dynamic environment. Embracing change involves not only accepting it but also harnessing its potential for growth. Navigating challenges with resilience is an essential companion to adaptability, allowing individuals to maintain their momentum even in the face of adversity.

## Thriving in a Dynamic Environment

Thriving in a dynamic environment requires a willingness to step out of one's comfort zone and welcome new possibilities. Embracing change means viewing it as an opportunity rather than a threat. It involves being open to different perspectives, ideas, and ways of doing things. By recognizing that change is a constant and inevitable part of life, individuals can position themselves to harness its potential benefits.

Moreover, adapting to change requires a flexible mindset that is receptive to learning and growth. Being willing to acquire new skills, update knowledge, and adjust strategies is key to remaining relevant and competitive. The capacity to pivot and redirect efforts when circumstances shift can lead to innovative solutions and unforeseen successes.

Adaptable individuals possess a flexible and forward-thinking mindset. They continuously seek to expand their skill set and knowledge base, positioning themselves to navigate shifting circumstances with confidence. Adapting to change requires being comfortable with ambiguity and having the willingness to step outside of one's comfort zone.

Furthermore, individuals who embrace change are not merely reactive; they are proactive in anticipating and preparing for shifts in their environment. They actively seek opportunities to learn, evolve, and innovate. This proactive stance allows them to seize new possibilities, drive progress, and stay ahead of the curve.

# Navigating Challenges with Resilience

Navigating challenges with resilience is the complementary aspect of embracing change. Resilience is the ability to bounce back from setbacks, adversity, and failures.
It involves maintaining composure under pressure, finding solutions in difficult situations, and not letting obstacles define one's path.

Resilience requires developing a strong sense of self-belief and a positive attitude. Instead of dwelling on failures, resilient individuals focus on the lessons learned and the potential for growth. They view challenges as temporary hurdles and remain committed to their goals, regardless of the difficulties they encounter.

Additionally, maintaining a growth mindset is integral to navigating challenges with resilience. Rather than viewing challenges as insurmountable obstacles, individuals with a growth mindset see them as stepping stones toward improvement. They embrace setbacks as valuable lessons and use these experiences to refine their strategies and approaches.

Furthermore, cultivating a support network is instrumental in building resilience. Surrounding oneself with mentors, friends, and colleagues who provide encouragement, guidance, and perspective can make navigating challenges more manageable. The collective wisdom and experiences of this network can offer new insights and solutions when facing adversity.

In conclusion, embracing change and adaptability is a dynamic approach to navigating the complexities of the modern world. It involves not only welcoming change but also leveraging it for growth and improvement. Paired with resilience, this mindset empowers individuals to overcome challenges and setbacks, emerging stronger and more determined.

By developing a flexible mindset and building resilience, individuals can not only thrive in a dynamic environment but also seize opportunities for personal and professional advancement.

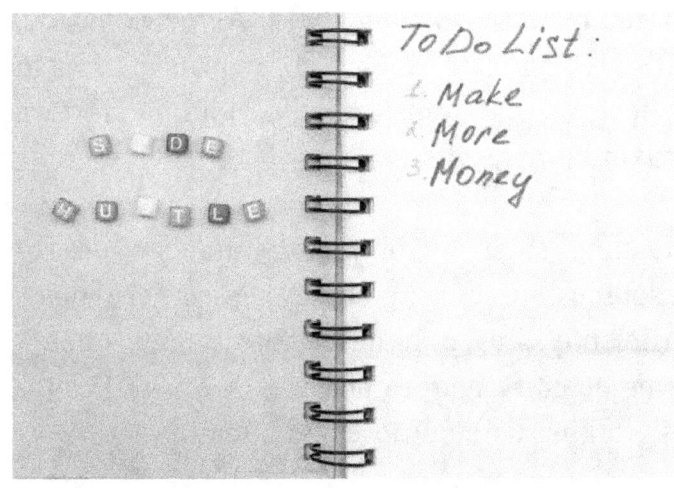

# CHAPTER 16

# CONCLUSION

In the journey to achieve success and fulfillment, the principles of hustling smart, not just hard, have emerged as a guiding light. Throughout this exploration, we've delved into various aspects of this mindset, from understanding the importance of efficiency and creating systems to achieving work-life harmony and managing stress. As we conclude, let's recapitulate these core principles and reflect on the transformative journey toward maximizing results.

Hustling smart involves the strategic use of resources, time, and energy to achieve goals efficiently. It's a mindset that values quality over quantity and emphasizes the significance of working with purpose and intention.

By understanding the importance of efficiency, individuals can optimize their processes, allocate resources wisely, and achieve more in less time.

Hustling smart revolves around the notion that success is not solely measured by the amount of effort exerted, but rather by the strategic application of that effort. We've learned that efficiency is the cornerstone of smart hustling, emphasizing the intelligent allocation of resources and time. Through streamlining processes, embracing automation, and leveraging productivity tools, we can optimize our workflows and unlock our full potential.

Creating systems and workflows is a cornerstone of hustling smart. By streamlining processes and embracing automation and productivity tools, individuals enhance their productivity and focus on high-impact tasks. The iterative approach to refining these systems ensures that they remain effective and adaptable, fostering a culture of continuous improvement.

Cultivating a winning mindset has emerged as a transformative principle on this journey. By overcoming self-doubt and limiting beliefs, we empower ourselves to pursue our goals with unwavering determination. Resilience and persistence have proven to be invaluable traits, allowing us to navigate challenges, setbacks, and failures with grace, learning from each experience and emerging stronger than before.

Work-life harmony is the art of seamlessly integrating work commitments with personal pursuits. Setting boundaries, embracing flexibility, and practicing self-care contribute to a balanced and fulfilling life. Avoiding burnout and managing stress are vital aspects of this harmony, ensuring that individuals can thrive in both their professional and personal spheres.

As we reflect on these principles, it's clear that the journey to maximizing results is a holistic one. It involves aligning our actions with our values, nurturing relationships, and nurturing ourselves. It's about finding the sweet spot between effort and balance, pushing ourselves to achieve while recognizing the importance of well-being.

The path to maximizing results is not without challenges, but the rewards are immeasurable. It requires self-awareness, discipline, and a willingness to adapt.
Each step taken in the direction of hustling smart contributes to a richer, more fulfilling life—one where accomplishments are met with a sense of purpose and satisfaction.

In the grand tapestry of life, hustling smart is the thread that weaves together our aspirations, actions, and outcomes. It's a reminder that success is not solely defined by the quantity of work put in, but by the quality of the journey taken. So, as we move forward, let's continue to embrace these principles, strive for efficiency, create systems, and seek that harmonious balance. In doing so, we embark on a transformative journey that leads to the maximization of results and the realization of our greatest potential.

**Dear Readers,**

I am truly humbled and grateful for your incredible support in purchasing and reading my book, "Hustle Smart; Not Hard." Your enthusiastic response and engagement have warmed my heart and affirmed the value of the message I aimed to convey.

It is a privilege to know that my words have resonated with you and perhaps even provided insights into a more efficient and fulfilling way of approaching life's challenges. Your dedication to personal growth and your willingness to embrace the concept of smart hustling inspire me deeply.

Each page of "Hustle Smart; Not Hard" was crafted with the intention of helping you navigate your journey with wisdom and purpose. Your decision to invest your time and energy in reading this book is a testament to your commitment to making positive changes in your life.

As you continue your pursuit of success and balance, remember that hustling smart involves not only the strategies outlined in the book but also your unique experiences and insights. Your journey is a dynamic and evolving one, and I am thrilled to have played a small role in it.

Thank you once again for your unwavering support. I look forward to hearing about your successes, challenges, and the many ways you apply the principles of smart hustling in your life. May you continue to thrive, achieve your goals, and find fulfillment in all that you do.

**With heartfelt gratitude,**

**[Ethan Yoder]**

www.ingramcontent.com/pod-product-compliance
Lightning Source LLC
Chambersburg PA
CBHW062333290526
45794CB00005B/2011

MAXIMIZING
EFFORTS
FOR
MAXIMUM
RESULTS

ISBN 9798856865973